I, VINCENT

PRINCETON ESSAYS ON THE ARTS

ADVISORY COMMITTEE: MONROE C. BEARDSLEY, EDWARD T. CONE,
HOWARD HIBBARD, EDMUND L. KEELEY, A. RICHARD TURNER

I, Vincent

Poems from the Pictures
of Van Gogh

By Robert Fagles

Princeton University Press
Princeton, New Jersey

Copyright © 1978 by Robert Fagles
Published by Princeton University Press, Princeton, New Jersey
In the United Kingdom: Princeton University Press, Guildford, Surrey

ALL RIGHTS RESERVED

Library of Congress Cataloging in Publication Data will
be found on the last printed page of this book

Publication of this book has been aided by the Paul Mellon Fund
of Princeton University Press

This book has been composed in Linotype Times Roman

Clothbound editions of Princeton University Press books are printed
on acid-free paper, and binding materials are chosen for strength
and durability

Printed in the United States of America
by Princeton University Press, Princeton, New Jersey

A previous version of "Crows over the Wheat Field" originally
appeared in *The Malahat Review*, 12 October 1969

For Lynne

Contents

Foreword

These poems are imitations of pictures by Van Gogh and often of his letters too. I have written them in the spirit with which he approached his masters, Rembrandt, Millet and Delacroix. They are translations, in other words, and they are very free. At times a poem will refer to a few works at once, while the introduction to the painter stands alone, and the conclusion suggests some later, modern works he might have valued. Although I refer mainly to his paintings rather than his letters, I have also borrowed and adapted certain passages from them. And the sequence of the poems is just as free; it is less a strict chronology of the pictures than a version, a draft, of the last ten years of Vincent's life when he became an artist.

The reproductions should serve simply as reminders of the originals themselves. They are now in various collections, acknowledged in the List of Illustrations. I owe more personal debts to Princeton University: to the Art Museum for preparing several prints, the Research Committee for sharing my expenses, and the staff of the University Press. Jan Lilly designed the book, illustrating (better than I had seen) the ties between the poems and the pictures; Jerry Sherwood joined my editors, Margot Cutter and Robert Brown, in offering me precision and support.

Many people have helped me with their kindness. My thanks to Richard Howard for his advocacy, his trust in the writing; to Mary Ann Caws and Jim Richardson for timely understanding; to Mike Keeley, Bill Meredith, and Ted Weiss for steady incentive; to David Lenson for that and criticism as well. To Patsy Chappell for the eye of the seahawk, warmth and faith. And to my mother who liked to look at pictures with me, especially Van Gogh's.

R. F.

List of Illustrations

I. FROM THE BORINAGE IN THE LOW COUNTRIES TO PARIS
July/August 1880–February 1888

And He went down to the mines the Black Country
there to tend the sick and preach the Gospel
test the light that rises in the dark

and perhaps by the age of thirty to return
with something to say and riper for the work

went down through the long shaft and left behind
the family legacy the traffickers in art
300 meters down and left his fathers
pastors conjuring Jesus from a text
and not a vision
                    and 500 meters down
below a land where there are no pictures
but the blackthorn hedge
engraves the snow like characters in Luke
he remembered always "When thine eye is single
thy whole body also is full of light"

and 700 meters down saw for the first time
the men who walk in darkness and the light
of the miner's lamp that cuts the night like diamonds
and the rows of miners in their cells like prisoners
no like bakers at their ovens filled with leaven
or weavers flourishing not on faith but labor
deep in that underworld beheld a world of life

and rose refreshed at the spring thaw
and watched the corn prodding up through the ice
and the play of light and dark on slagheaps
reminiscent of van Ruysdael and van Rijn
                              and one night
on the high ground when rain and galewinds
whipped the shaft   Marcasse the Common Grave
beheld that black scaffold radiant in the lightning
breasting clear of the flood like Noah's ark

3

beheld but could not express
not by preaching shipwreck and resurrection
bargaining with the owners of the mines or
swabbing burns with shirting soaked in oil
but was discharged for zeal   zeal

and wept through the nights with hunger and remorse
and late into those nights began to draw
because a Rembrandt was better than a sermon
and began to sign the drawings Vincent
"to send a brotherly message to the wretched"
to be like them
                        he began to draw quite late
not that the talent for it was overwhelming
but the desire was—
there was so much to see   so much in motion
        men and women moving to their tasks and
deep in the beechleaves glints of copper flickering
pollard willows writhing as in grief
                                    and learned
to look through the lashes and beheld
beyond the rifts the breaks
masses of color merging
                        rough shapes
of the world of Eve and Adam growing human
yes and a longing rose to seize those figures
not in their sin or innocence but their vigor
strong as they were before God thundered
Thou shalt not and split us into atoms—

                                        Cain
in the wilderness would be his brother's keeper
restore Eden or certain acres of it
not through works of faith
but pictures charged
with the lightning of this life because
"to hope for better times must not be a feeling
but an *action* in the present"
                                    but a wall stood
between what he felt / what he in fact could do
and to break through with a draftsman's fist
preferred a carpenter's pencil for its roughness
and sensing with Millet that art is combat—
work for stevedores
that can take the skin off a man's back—
relished the enterprise and said "I am seeking
I am striving—I am in it with all my heart"

And resolved to spare himself not at all
(the work would count and not the length of days)
and wrote "I have walked on the earth for thirty years
and out of gratitude want to leave some souvenir
in the shape of drawings or pictures
not made to please a certain trend in art
but to express a genuine human feeling"
                                    And believed
"Whosoever shall save his life shall lose it"—
an evangelist of art who loved the storm
who worked with the thunder's fury
would grasp the great black silhouette of this world
with a few strokes of light and let the rest be dark—
would be the lightning while the lightning lasts

Studies, Sketches:
The Hague

MINERS' WIVES CARRYING SACKS OF COAL

Snow, vast wastes of snow
                              interminable
far as the eye can see, the clouds dense
but there before him, women, backs bending . . .
(he bends too)
hard as it looks, the way they carry coal
sacks strapped to the forehead breaks the weight.

They bear the burden, small caravan moving out.
They keep a spark alive to the next day
(keep a spark alive)
to the next railhead
                              next milestone
                                                  (someday
could the work resemble something out of Breughel?
Try. Too soon. Not yet.)

CARPENTER'S WORKSHOP, SEEN FROM THE
ARTIST'S WINDOW

First light. Just picture him
perched at his attic window,
early as four in the morning, studying,
with his perspective frame, the meadows,
the carpenter's workshop down below . . .
they are lighting the fires for morning coffee,
the cottages stir,
the first workman loiters into the yard.

And over his head a patrol of pigeons
veering along the chimneys, past the roofs
a sweep of lush green a line below the horizon—
lines of the roofs and gutters shooting into the distance
like arrows from a bow, drawn without hesitation.

Draw without hesitation, can he?
Carpenter's pencil first,
a quick wash for shadow.
Bird that flies. Window open.
Man working—quickness.

SIEN'S DAUGHTER: PROFILE

Sunday morning. He watches the little girl.
She is her mother's daughter.
The old misery cannot be erased,
ingrained, darker than his charcoal . . .
her shawl smudged with soot.

  "Little Polly Flinders
    sat among the cinders"
                              Towsled hair,
circle under the eye, her mother's eye.
Observant, wary, live.

There is no such thing as an old woman.
No such thing as the timelessness of a moment,
only a moment of timelessness—

Oh God, she'd say, there is no God.
But there is life. And at times, love.

THE PADDEMOES, THE JEWISH QUARTER

Cordoned off from the New Church by iron grating,
potholed streets and poplars strict as sentries,
he draws them now, the dead of night,
shadows passing into his . . .
        into the clouds of autumn
slender chimneys, peaked roofs, the elegant
fragile mansions of the Chosen drift like smoke.

THE FORGE

soot-black hood   big hook
of the damper overhead
        good bed of coals
light through a foundry window
beak of the anvil gleaming
tongs at an ingot white-hot
blacksmith ramrod stiff
              To work, Vincent—
reach for the balanced hammer   strike
leverage all in the wrist   strike
with the grain of the iron
the flow lines   *strike*
till the lines come clear
from the first cast comes latch
mattock   ax
          Beat the thing into being
file the flashings
then anneal it screeching steam

Black metal—temper true

Weaver with Loom

Huge grimy frame, oak, ribs protruding—
lifeless, dwarfing the life inside it
a spirit caged and dreaming
   absent-minded
        moving slowly
warpbeam breastbeam slowly
the old man begins his weaving
sheds and picks and beats
   clogs working the treadles
   hooks and the griff-bar lifting
shedding picking and beating in
   hand at the driver dark with sweat—
   a light knock
   and the rapier shuttle flying fast
   as the weft builds the warp goes under
shedding picking and beating in
   as the weaver's fingers fly
   my days are swifter than his shuttle—
forth from our black frame come rolling white
and glistening bolts bright bolts of cloth

13

The Potato-Eaters   *i*

Nightfall under the lamplight   now they take their meal

salt of the earth they are
                              earth-born earth-bound
the hands of the earth
                              the furrowed hands
that hold the plow
                         hold fork and brazen pot
their backs bending
                         facing each other
boar's head   crowhead
   head of a fawn among the thorns
and the eyes bright   enduring
                         filled with hope and a hunger
one pours coffee
                    dark in the white cups
one serves potatoes
              white as the hoar frost on the ground
and one supper leads to the next
                              and that the next
the hands that work the earth
                              reach out together
men women together
                         nursed by the food they grow
the body and the blood of earth

But will they share their sacrament with me?

I have sought them often at end of day.
The moors dark, last of the sun
a closing wound in the west.
An exile, sought their hovels often,
low-thatched roof, a light in the window—
door opens, enter. And while they eat
I sketch and paint

               figures, heads, hands
so dark in the lamplight,
       hardly see the palette . . .
ivory black? Too flat. Mix Prussian blue
with burnt sienna, a little vermilion;
make your black shimmer, catch the light
in the darkness.

               Keep the miner's faith—
not father's faith, old preacher,
too otherworldly. Work is faith.
I've only one wish: to paint peasants,
keep a hand on the plough and cut my furrow.

    "Paint them with the earth they sow . . ."
     Millet. I follow him, now father's gone.

—Sick of the *boredom* of civilization.
Better here. Feel alive here.
Good to live in the winter deep in snow,
deep in the yellow leaves in fall, in summer
deep in the ripe corn, deep in the grass in spring—
good to be with the mowers, the peasant girls,
in summer always under the big sky overhead,
in winter beside the open fire, and feel
it always has been, always will be so.

Sentimental? Perhaps, but not at this point.
A prodigal, I begin to find myself . . .
painting *is* like a home.
Working back to the fatherland, the people.
Paint them with the earth they sow.

"Laborers all,

we suffer in this life—laborers, we are blessed."

iii

Thank God for the night that comes upon us;
   darkness breeds the light.
Thank God for the hail, the lashing rain;
   the cyclone strides with power.
Thank God for the aching in the marrow;
   pain dilates the pores.
Thank God for the grim defiant fist;
   resentment makes us strong.
Thank God for the hatred in our lives;
   the more we hate the more we can revere.
Thank God for the oblivion of his Heaven—
   we must love our lives.

Thank God

for the earth we are, the earth we will become;
our flesh is dark and fertile as the earth.

Women

Make for the docks at Antwerp, seadogs, dancehalls,
women, women—the well-toned flesh like honey.
Get my hands full of their flesh,
possess them, paint them, *both*—

                             Many women,
a few handsome, the finest of them homely.
One out of Goya danced in her black silks,
hugging a rich captain,
              waltzing the old way—
ugly as sin, irresistible.

(My thoughts are full of Rembrandt, Hals.)

And the girl I took to model, many times,
and the one I did for her she liked the most.
A head life-size, and the dark mane tumbling,
cinched with a carmine ribbon
red as wine, the warmth, the life of wine.
"For me, the champagne has lost its sparkle,
only fills me with tears," she says . . .
I think I see, I try
for something voluptuous, slightly damaged.

(When I paint peasants I want them to be peasants.
When I paint whores I want them to be whores.
Rembrandt's *Head of a Harlot*:
he caught it all so well, the mysterious smile,
the gravity he alone possesses—magician of magicians.)

Paris . . . I can see her still,
arranged at a table at the Tambourin,
    evanescent across the gaslights
the din, the laughter, the long high kick
I see an aging model lovely still
    highlights wavering over her bodice
scarlet feathers flaming over her black hair
cigarette burning lower
                            always waiting
for someone new
                        (I decorated her walls once;
the café went bankrupt, she withheld my work,
whatever I couldn't salvage in a pushcart.
Bear no grudge—needs to be top dog in business.
If, to get on, she tramples on my toes, all right;
when I see her now
she doesn't trample on my feelings.
Something remains between us, over her features
the old smile seems to play . . .)

    "The love of art destroys real love."

No, Richepin, not exactly.

Something remains.
Shimmer of silk
                touch of scarlet
                                a certain smile

Fishing in Spring,
Probably near the
Pont Levallois

first spring haze   shimmering
down through willow green
shower of light
                    kaleidoscopic
spray of a rainbow   light over water
drifting still   craft adrift
dips   lifts and eddies
going nowhere
line falls slack
          arm of the bridge
slipping down through the willows
  not a breath   hypnotic
the lovely misting light
and the random drop
              pearls to a diamond
                                pales
the will a ballet of velleities
through veils I have touched
a part of it all
                    but not myself
my image blurs in the shallows
nodding
              dissolving   water-
          skimmer all on the surface
lose myself on the surface
and the rarer catch
lolls at bottom
              Vincent
a shadow pooling darker   Vincent
glints   darts
              deeper than I can go

**View from Montmartre
near the Upper Mill**

On through the mist
    meandering
            mother-of-pearl
on along the files of lampposts
fencing wire-fine
wavering near a pavilion
               high as dunes
and the great swirling sea of the city
all before me
          soft whorls of mist
luminous   blurring
           but for the mist
I might make out the Louvre
the Invalides, the dome and spire
the impossible aspiration testing Heaven—
                   Never,
lost in the mist I am, but always at my back
I feel the immense mill grinding,
sails in the wind blown tight—

Power of home, dark Holland, row me on
through the mesmerizing light of Paris
on the horizon someday let me see
new world   new Eden   now
I cannot see a thing

**Père Tanguy
the Paint-Grinder**

The Revolution lives in you, old soldier—
battle-hard from the lost Commune of '71,
you carry the colors now for us,
Seurat, Signac, and me.
                              Your worker's hands
clasped, almost reverent (not like a martyr,
more like Socrates with that wife,
a rabid bitch from the Institut Pasteur);
you adore an art, some say, you cannot understand.

Over your burly frame they rise behind you:
Hokusai's view of Fujiyama hung in mist,
a wisp of an actress done by Yoshitora . . .
a few strokes of the brush and she has breath.

Understand—why shouldn't you understand?
You with your friendly ugly face,
grizzled, ruddy with life.
Your eyes are clear, they say "Be simple—
the man who lives on more than 75 centimes a day
is a rascal. Put your blood in your work
and let the colors come!"
                              Red as your lips,
red, green, gold as the hat across your brow,
I outline you in red—
you glow among our paintings like Marat.

Lend us your arsenal of colors, Père Tanguy,
and we will give you work. We are your stock,
let our revolution come—
triumphant as your crimson, ever-new.

**Self-Portrait
in Front of the Easel**

Palette in hand, at the scaffold my easel—
Paris, city of light, make me a painter!

Light, bridges, still lifes, mills, streets,
I've tried them all. Your alleys wind me
back and back into myself. Staring into
the imbecile blank canvas staring back at me,
vacant as life itself.
                                        Stop.
Look in the mirror.
Step in, act, and build up—*ruins*. No,
a torso, head, block out the head
                                                    the hair
like a scarecrow, forehead wrinkled, stiff.

                    corn man   clay man   man of flesh

Back and forth, mirror to canvas, capture the image,
flesh pale gray, I see the face of . . .
Death in van Eeden's book—
Suicide, this.
                        Stop transcribing.
Work against the grain.
Work *through* the mirror image.
Never things as they are but as you feel them,
not the hand but the gesture
                    palette held like a shield
                        brushes like a quiver full of arrows—
not the measurements of the head but the expression,
under the brows the eyes deep green.
                                        Face in the mirror,
death's-head, you want to express
strenuous sorrow, not some weak-kneed despair?
Then reach far, deeply, tenderly—notwithstanding
your so-called roughness, perhaps because of it.

You and I, two men becoming one?
A rough man blossoming like a plant,
a dark man burning.

I am looking out at you,
my brother—look into my eyes.

I see two brothers walking through The Hague . . .
one says, "I must keep up a certain standing,
stay in business, never become a painter."
And the other, "I am getting like a dog,
and the future makes me uglier, rougher—
'a certain poverty' will be my lot—
but I will be a painter."
                              Strange,
I can still see those brothers in childhood,
both fresh to the world of pictures, see them
near the Rijswijk mill, or walking to Chaam
some winter morning across the snowy heath,
feeling, thinking, *believing* so alike—
Are they the same two brothers?

Can this portrait form a bond between us?
One rough, one smooth. One the painter,
one the entrepreneur, each other's keeper:
"I give you pictures, if they are worth their salt"—
"I give you support, and half the work is mine."
You and I—with luck, one flesh, one bone?

Think of the last walk of the two de Goncourts,
the last days of old Turgenev too.
Sensitive, subtle, intelligent as women;
sensitive to their own suffering, what's more,
yet always full of life, alert to themselves—
no frozen stoicism, no contempt for life.
These fellows, I tell you, they die as women die.
No fixed idea about God. No abstractions.
Always based on the firm ground of life itself,
rooted in that alone.
                              Our bond is art,
my brother, strong as the likeness
growing on this canvas.

Painting *is* inborn,
Theo, but not as most suppose. No,
you must put your hands out, reach for it,
grasp it—painfully obvious, I know:
only by painting one becomes a painter.

Here I am, palette in hand, a static image . . .
captured? Not really. Suspended, waiting,
painting—I am painting.
See, one works. What next? I don't know.
Should be moving, getting clear of the sight
of so many painters who as men disgust me.
God, how many have grown desperate in Paris,
calmly, rationally, logically, rightly desperate.
Labyrinthine alleys . . . Paris a gorgeous ruin—
break off!

Go back to the land,
get good soil under your feet

corn man   clay man   man of flesh

The first of the morning hits my blue peasant blouse,
it warms my neck, my temples. Out of the darkness
of my features flash a thousand points of light!
The sun and the citron yellow on my palette
coruscate, catch fire—

South, I must go south
until I catch that fire in my hands—

II. ARLES IN PROVENCE

February 1888–May 1889

The Coaches of Tarascon

Travel light—the coaches, look,
like sloops at a rakish angle
set to sail.
              The iron horse
may drive you into oblivion, old relics,
here you stand at the caravansary
if I can only paint
your fleeting lines, scarlet, green—
varnish your wheels a high gloss of black,
your tarpaulin rubbed with oil, lantern like a moon.

I can smell the women, the leather, the dank straw,
hear the bells and barking, see the stallions
plunging south—
    Mount the ladder, draw it up,
the voice of the old *diligence* of Tarascon,
clear as a post horn calling Tartarin,
      "Drive me, little hunter—
harness a team of four and crack your whip.
Provence, a highway paved with dreams is waiting—
                    you and I will travel like the wind!"

**Vincent's Bedroom
in Arles**

Even at rest the world is moving toward me.
Perspective is never given, it is earned.

Simply my own bedroom.
This well-lit place where I awake . . .
there are no shadows here, but the room
and all its things are closing in
unless I hold them off.

Here is the floor, planing toward me,
tiles go red to green. I fit them flush
for a good footing.
                              Here's my bed,
rugged poplar, yellow as butter—
I make it lean toward me, more inviting,
plump the pillows, heap the quilts, deep red.

And I brace the two chairs, their seats
are rush and waiting, firm.

A washstand, glass, carafe,
my stiff brush, soap and water.

And the walls slope inward, hung
with a landscape, a woman's face and mine.

Here is a mirror. Here the window opens.
Morning light drifts in.
I have framed my room in white.
Wonderful, how all things come to rest.

Sunflowers

Thank God that I can rise with the sun
reap these flowers rising with the sun

but rush they go so quickly
do them in one rush   you must
the buds dense with the gold
opening firmly   paint them
ochre to chrome to gold
the petals curl
    rounding out now
quick before they wither
take the thrust of the stalk
the head flung back
                    exultant
petals stretching stronger
the center
stronger now take hold
of the big shag bloom
                    the hurling rays
before they burn into umber go to seed
if I can make these flowers mine
            their prime my prime
     their corona my dark heart
is bursting green to gold
               God help me
flower with these flowers
with all their husk and sudden glory
yes I fling my arms to the sun while there is time
I rise with these great flowers dying into life

Self-Portrait:
A mon ami Paul G.

Japan of the south, Arles, bright Eden Garden—
they are the real infidels who don't adore this sun!

Look in the mirror. Could I be a simple bonze
and worship Eternal Buddha face to face?
Mantled in brown, my head shaved,
I send this portrait on to you, Gauguin;
you sent me yours—

        A powerful ruffian, you seem,
red with the hot blood of Jean Valjean,
and the lava of your glance
pulses with inner kindness too. Poor victim,
prisoner who retaliates only by doing good.
"*Les Misérables,*" your motto for us all.

                    True,
we are both rejected, both violent men,
but I think my portrait holds its own with yours;
just as grave but somehow less despairing.
See, I am almost colorless, ashen-gray
yet there is a brightness too,
and it's not an easy shade to get,
I blended malachite green with orange;
I paint not only with color but with denial,
renunciation, and at times a broken heart—
lashing myself, forging a style of my own
before the volcano of Gauguin erupts in Arles.

And I have these fainting spells . . .
I've thought, at times, I might go mad.
(I always remember Emile Wauters' rendering
of Hugo van der Goes, the mad Flemish painter;
he entered a monastery at thirty-five . . .
I see him there in his novice robes,
hands clenched, eyes glazed
in a catatonic stare, transfixed
by the choirboys and placid, graceful priest
who weave their hymns around him—quite mad.)

41

Well I could work myself to the limit too.
Not into persecution mania like yours,
Gauguin. I could go mad with Eternity—
serve my Maker, manic with all the modesty
of the Chosen.
                    I could go Japanese.
The Japanese artist spends his time—how?
Gauging the distance between the earth and moon?
No. Poring over the policies of Bismarck?
No, he studies a single blade of grass
but the grassblade leads him on to draw the plant
and then the wheel of the seasons, then the clean sweep
of the open country, then the beasts of the field and
then the human figures. So he weathers his life,
exchanging portraits with his brothers.

O Gauguin, come south—the garden of God!
A brotherhood of painters in the south.
Japanese painters, new primitives.
Bold flat planes of color.
Outlines sharp.
Execution swift as lightning.
The work like breathing—Japanese.
Because his nerves are finer, feelings stripped.

I begin to disabuse myself of Paris.
The din and the intrigue, the rice-powder,
superficial halos—Ai, the gaiety,
the sheer dogma of gaiety . . .
Impressionism,
a million stipples of light—
enough of atoms. Let it all cohere!

Let the light come forth from deep inside
so all can feel the light—
                              I slant my eyes,
oriental eyes, but ablaze with my own will.
The more I efface myself the more I am myself,
Japanese and still myself:
                              "A man's character
shines forth in every one of his brushstrokes"—
this painting, let me live up to this painting!
Let the emaciation of my flesh sublime
into the highlights of my brow,
into pure luminous spirit—
Help me, Lord.

             I remember Michelet on Socrates:
"he was born a real satyr, but through devotion, toil
and self-mortification, stripping off his follies,
he so transformed himself that when,
that last day he stood before his judges facing death,
some indefinable quality, some godhead stood out in him,
some heavenly radiance that lit the Parthenon."

                              Je suis sain d'esprit
                              Je suis le Saint-Esprit

Harvest

in the beginning   fields of light   fences vineyards wheat

and the eye moving left to right   reading the book of nature
words made things made fences vineyards wheat

and the world a study of God that has not yet come off
and we must not judge the artist   not if we're fond of the artist
not if we know the first draft of a master when we see one

vineyards ladders wagons hayricks wheat

not if we take up pen and ink and the white page of the morning
quill-pen   reed-pen   close to the things themselves
reading writing
                    stroke   stroke aslant   a stalk
                              a grassblade / wheatstem
words the roots of it all
                    scroll of the vinestock
                              a wet scything slash
and the long even rows the immemorial meadows m's on end

calligraphy of the world   the signatures of God   writing drawing
and there are times I cannot tell if I am writing drawing
or doing both
                    I think this is a map   cartography   all too flat
until I get my vision into it   work with color   the clear strain
of vineyard green   wagon blue   hayrick bronze with harvest

work with the men at harvest   strange the labor does not weary
it refreshes yes I am launching out with color   onto a huge canvas

over the gold ricks the wheat fields rolling green to gold over
in endless repetition stretching toward the horizon like the sea

the earth as oceanic as the sea   but not the sea as a sailor friend
points out   as level overwhelming and infinite   but inhabited look

the men at the ladders   vintners dressing vines   and the houses
stucco white in the noon glare   the tile roofs stark orange

inhabited by the spirit of the place   the blue of his sky
bleached green with the heat   his scorching yellows pitched so high
you can frame his work in gold   Cézanne
                                                              I work toward Cézanne
the god of the harvest working over the ricks and vines and houses
on to the distant line of cypress   on to the ruined abbey Montmajour
where the monks reclaimed the flatlands from the fens and made them green

wedding them to the vines the wheat the far Alpilles and coping
the mountain ridges spread the heavens
                                                         never tiring with these hands
apprentice now to the master drawing even with himself at last
writing drawing illuminating the book of nature
                                                         close to scripture
in the beginning always working   never finished   they who sow in tears
shall reap in joy the fields of light these growing sheaves of wheat

**Boats on the Beach
at Saintes-Maries**

free—
                    the first ocean morning
                                          sea   sand
and the fishing skiffs
                              a bright lift of wind
wash of foam in the beach groove
                                        hissing turquoise clear
and the dunes buoy
                          dun to buff
                                        undulating under the hulls
drawn up like terns at rest
                                a bowsprit beaking red
and the stern of one says Friendship
over the waterline
                          ultramarine
                                        the strakes curve
I love their lines
                        simplicity of their lines
the clean wood and the wonder
                                      quick before the crews
come down for launching
                                    draw one down to the edge
the mast stepped
                        halyards taut
                                    and the gaff branching
set your sails
                    head out now
                                    master the ropes now
with an expert hand
                          it would be easy
                                          craft agile

rigid   swift
                    under the azure running free
                                        such strain
such play
            give in to a headwind
                                rein it in till
you and the craft are one
                        shearing the sea line
                                        on out
spindrift   whitecaps
                        vision limitless
                                    Africa in the offing
wings of the seahawk
                    glinting wings of the wind

**Vincent's Chair
with His Pipe**

all I work with is myself
my own empty chair
4 legs cut trim
ladderback straight
and a rush seat tight
but empty
                there are
so many empty chairs
and soon there will be more
soon nothing but empty chairs
my father's chair I painted once
and now I paint my own
standing apart   a spirit
restless hovering over
a chair abandoned
                        but
I place my pipe and pouch
tobacco shagcut brown
on the seat and plant
the chairlegs deep
in the clay tiles
paint a box of maple
banked with flowers
I call Vincent
a lifeless chair the air
I breathe is Vincent
                        all
my absence is a presence
all my passing is
a standing fast

The Postman Roulin

He poses a moment, ill at ease;
I keep him from his rounds,
bearing the word of others hour by hour.

Soldier of time, his uniform is blue:
gold frogs at the cuff, his visor marked
with the regiment he serves, the Post—
fresh decorations won and worn in peace.

Fortitude, and such a homely face.
Snub nose, thick forest of beard,
like a satyr, Socrates, or Père Tanguy . . .
but his eyes shine
with the son his wife just bore him.

(Treats me like a son too,
an old sergeant fond of a young recruit.)

I've watched you sing the "Marseillaise," Roulin.
Your voice comes through like a cradlesong
or a distant trumpet-call that echoes '89;
that's it, I am watching '89—not next year
but 99 years ago. You terrible Republican,
you loathe the Republic, doubt the principle itself
but not the comradeship, the warmth.
                                        I paint you
as I know you, soul of trust, dear friend.
I receive your message all but framed in words:
"The older we get the harder it gets.
Nothing will improve. Well, head high—
no fear of tomorrow. Think of me."

**Portrait of
the Artist's Mother**

Photography, demon of reproduction—I despise it.
So black-and-white, this tintype of mother,
unbearable.
                          Too reminiscent of the past,
the rift within herself: part love, part dogma,
starched as a nun in the parsonage at Etten.
Reminiscent of the growing rift between us—
how she clings to the life hereafter,
clings to the first Vincent,
the infant dead, my double, my accuser.

Mother, you are so distant
I will paint you with a vengeance,
draw you from memory . . .
                                    three years gone,
1,000 kilometers out of Holland,
south beneath this sun—and all I see
is violet, somber, blossoming into yellow,
strict lips
          glistening into a smile
                          your brow expansive, blond

Of the life hereafter I know nothing, mother,
but when I paint you what I feel is yellow,
lemon yellow, the halo of the rose.

**Old Shepherd
in Provence**

Frightening, how he recalls my father—
Patience Escalier,
a seasoned hand at the wild white horses
of the Camargue, the vineyards of La Crau.

He rises out of the darkness, leans toward me;
his smock blue, crown of his hat yellow,
leathery features bronze,
rubbed gold in the shadows going bronze.
Best of the old gardeners rooted in the earth.

He *is* the earth, sun-burnt, sun-whipped,
swept by the lacerating winds—
                              He is the sky,
the lightning vivid as white-hot iron, his lips,
his cheekbones storm-flashed with orange.
                                        Terrible
in the furnace of the ardors of the harvest—
blazing heart of the south.

                              But not his eyes . . .
luminous, tender, grave, they seem to say,
"Why paint me, son, what good am I to you?"
Let the warmth of your generations be upon me—
ripen the work of my hands upon me, father,
full and ripe as Adam in the fall.

**The Rhone River
at Night**

Difficult things, it does me good to try them.
But it cannot stop a dreadful yearning for—
shall I say the word? Religion.
Then I go out at night and paint the stars.

I reach for the infinite clear above me.
After a bracing walk along the shore,
the night and the stars are neither gay nor sad,
they're breathtaking . . .
I paint in the darkness like a perfect fool,
a crazy halo of candles in my hatband—
I am a Roman candle burning out.

                              But now
the feel of the oils increases in the dark,
unguents . . . undulant
sand dunes sifting mauve
and the river gliding out to sea
        the long arc of the sea wall gliding

                                        Arles in darkness
gaslights caught in the waters rippling bronze
and the night sky vaulting blue
                        an ocean of cobalt overhead
                                    and the Great Bear ramping high
his stars burn white burn rose   burn lapis sapphire
watch, I am working into the opal's black fire—

Carried away   the picture comes in a trance
I dream beyond the Bear
                            beyond the pole
                                        beyond

This side of death we see one hemisphere only,
and beyond? I can't tell
but when I look at the stars I always dream
as I dream upon a map, the towns, the black dots—
these points of light in the heavens,
how to reach them?

If we take the express to get to Tarascon
we take death to reach a star.

Woman of Arles

The more I look at her the more I quicken.
And I thought the heat had leeched the life
out of Provence, her women brittle, sickly.
Not at all—look at them long enough
the old charm revives.
                                    The hair and bodice
        perfectly raw Prussian blue,
                    her fichu eggshell white

Strong silhouette, serene and self-possessed

Against a background golden as the wheat
looking up from her book a moment
                                    face in full repose
she looks toward a future golden as the wheat

Profile of eternity, your life is on the line
Mine too, I begin to love you very much

(And a soldier friend has his techniques,
as many Arlésiennes as he could want;
but he can't paint them, poor man,
he can only impale them with his sex.)

I went to see her months later,
down with the same attacks that level me
and an early change of life. She seemed a crone,
an old grandfather. Even this canvas
deteriorates and flakes—I slashed her on
in less than an hour.
                                    Still her eye is young.
The best revenge is painting well.

A Bugler of the Zouave Regiment

Death is a Zouave bugler—
Death the mercenary camping at my door.

A man of action dressed to kill—
brings out the soldier in me,
irresistible . . .
the bolero jacket smart enamel blue,
stars at the heart, the braiding burnished,
under an emerald sash the trousers flaring wide—

    A silken, savage sweep of crimson slashed with red
        the body of death a red slouch of power in reserve—

Drawing with color now, the colors clash.
Must get the ring of the bugle in my colors.
This painting is a dangerous business,
take your life in your hands to capture him,
engage him—look, he slaps his thighs,
shoulders toward you,
    black hair cropped and the head bobbing
        eye of the panther
            panther's taut intensity
                coiled to spring—

The Night Café

A sweet haunt of the damned
where every step says welcome.

                Come,
we'll pick our way among the tables,
empty chairs and drifters . . .
the bar is waiting (calvados, absinthe,
colorless mother's milk that clouds and kills)
and a billiard table flat as a mortuary's slab,
and he waits too, his coat a lurid green,
the proprietor keeps his vigil, nods,
"Come in now, make yourself at home"—
                    We will,
where the gaslights throb, halos pulse
with the pulses in your veins,
enflame the walls, the red chamber—
this is the heart's chamber
                  I feel the walls
go blood-red, contract and pound, dilate   pound
peristaltic against the ceiling, red against green,
emerald envy clashing with scarlet anger—
                I can feel it with color—
     fear with rage, you with me where a man
might drown, go mad or rush to murder—

Gaslights flare
        senegal yellow
                floorboards sweep me on
                      headlong on
     the hands of the clock race midnight
it is time
the curtains part
infernal corridor
ends
devil's furnace
             sulfur
                flash-fire—
heart's igniting, feel it, taste it, paint it—

Draw your knife and cut!

    Palette knife, cut through the powers of darkness—

**Self-Portrait
with Bandaged Ear
and Pipe**

Mad I am not mad I am a painter—

               "If thine ear offend thee, cut it off"

Look at yourself now . . . face of the butcher,
fresh dressing white from the temples to the neck,
your pipe still burning. No, not mad at all,
just worked to the breaking-point—
to hit that pitch of yellow late last summer
cost you a little frenzy.
                     We painters have our work.
Shut me up with the mad or *let* me work,
with a few precautions . . . I am thinking now
of frankly accepting the role of madman,
as Degas took on the role of notary—
                      O dear God,
I lack the strength . . . too many roles to play.

          I am the matador of Arles I am the victim—
            one clean stroke of the knife
          I cut the ear from the sacrificial bull
          I offer the bloody trophy up to her—

WE WHO ARE ABOUT TO DIE SALUTE YOU!

I am the sword in the loins—sex that burns like death

I am I am—
                  The Ripper of Tarascon!—
        I graze the carotid artery, take the ear
     to Rachel, whore, meat in a butcher's shop—
never, a sister of charity
                and I her child . . .
Rachel, the voice we heard in Rama, "lamentation,
and weeping, and great mourning, Rachel weeping
for her children, and would not be comforted,
because they are not."

i

But I am I am—
this part of me into your safekeeping I entrust—
Help me, hold me. "Verily I say unto you
you will remember me."

I am the Christmas child,
dear mother, yes, and in this our last reunion
every crevice of Zundert filters back
in memory . . . I begin to see the grave, the stone
of the infant Vincent, read the inscription:

LET THE LITTLE CHILDREN COME TO ME
FOR OF SUCH IS THE KINGDOM OF GOD

Christmas

it is always Christmas—a child's paradise
maturing into a nightmare,
   livid as mistletoe against the oak,
      alienation amidst a host of strangers—
here in the midst of life we are in death
in the midst of Arles, green Eden Garden
it is the Garden of Olives I have found
and the whispers will not stop
I cut the ear of Malchus the high priest
and still the hiss of betrayal will not stop—

Gethsemane!

Features of Judas flickering through the olives,
clear-cut in the monumental canvas of Bernard
I see Gauguin . . .

I trailed you through the square
I sought you through the nights to make you stay
my voice a razor glinting in the dark
pleading for help

and you, you did my portrait—
it is I, but I gone mad and now you've fled,
the murderer slinking back to his banks in Paris
like Napoleon safe from Egypt,
leaving his diehard regiments in the ditch,
abandoning our outpost in the south—

Gauguin, the little tiger of Impressionism,
deserting his wife and cubs for Martinique.

There is virginal power in that man, true,
coupled with all the instincts of a savage—
in Gauguin blood and sex lord it over ambition,
over what you have in abundance, my good brother,
decency, and conscience, Theo—and self-denial.

At six I wash myself in the coal-bin,
practice Biblical mortifications.

"If thine ear offend thee, cut it off and cast it from thee . . .
better to enter into life with one ear, maimed,
than be cast into hell with two."

HELLFIRE—SWORD OF THE SUN!

First killing, then healing;
so the saying goes.

scar—ultimate clarity

"Suffer ye thus far.
And he touched his ear, and healed him."

ii

Theo,
good apostle, you have your life to live.
Marriage may sever you from me,
cut my support . . . unnerving, but Amen.
And not before I pay my debts to you,
or try. I throw myself in the work—
this portrait is for you.
"So much for hope," you say,
"we must accept the disasters of reality." *Amen.*

The background red. A workman's jacket green.
Red against green, like the features of Gauguin,
but forest green growing from scarlet anger—
I will make my peace.
                              My ear is bandaged,
pipe is burning. Never let the fire go out,
I keep it burning, not for heroics, martyrdom,
just the art of survival. (You remember
Dickens' prescription against suicide?
A glass of wine, a piece of bread, some cheese,
and a pipe to smoke your whack.) I have my work
cut out for me. The stroke of the brush
blocking out my features . . .
still alive, I still have my faith:
the refusal to make murderers of the living.

And I've a pinch of potassium bromide
to muffle the screaming in my ear,
reduce the terror to a common nightmare.
Madness is common here. Everyone
in Provence is mad, they reassure me.
And madness is a good deal less exclusive.
Even salutary. The camaraderie of the mad—
we, the happy possessors of shattered hearts.

        iii

I am a common man. A few highlights.
Fleshtones healthy, glance (almost) steady.

"—See more with imagination," said Gauguin.
Perhaps, but it's enchanted territory, comrade,
and you're soon brought up against a granite wall:
reality. I see what *is*. I accept it.
I am looking straight in the mirror;
I have no more illusions.
                              A trooper's cap
protects my head. A soldier of fortune
somewhat marked, campaigning in the south.

"Come to the tropics," said Gauguin.
I'm too old, my friend.
(And with an ear put on in papier-mâché
too much a thing of cardboard for the journey.)
What's more, with this green plot of mine
who needs the tropics? Primitive enough
right here, the land of the living,
fugitives from Eden.

I am a worker. In the sweat of my face
I eat my bread

corn man   clay man   man of flesh

Dust I am. To dust return. Have no more
illusions . . . none except my work.

                                    Dear brother,
I know so well what I want, sometimes I really know:
in life, in painting too, I can do without God,
easily, but I cannot—not in this condition—
go without something larger than myself.

No more illusions, none except my work.

Gauguin and I understand each other down deep,
and if we are a little mad, what of it?
Aren't we artists enough to quash those rumors
with a brush? Everyone will have his neurosis
someday soon, St. Vitus' dance, something else.
And don't we have the antidote? In Delacroix,
in Berlioz, and Wagner? That artist madness
even in us—that antidote, I tell you,
lend it a measure of good will,
it's ample compensation.

And what does it prove, day in, day out?
Ambition—lust for glory dies away
but the heart beats the same, beating
with the past of our buried fathers, beating
sane and strong with the generations still to come.

I have no more illusions, none except my work.
I am the painting while the painting lasts.

Sane because I only cut an ear.

III. FROM SAINT-RÉMY TO AUVERS NEAR PARIS
May 1889–May/July 1890

**A Passage at
St. Paul's Hospital**

halls down how many halls down rows of cells
where the monks did battle with the devil
now the mad confront themselves
                                        down
hallways tunneling like a vein
I hear the voices throbbing
brother inmates take my hand
we are Samaritans and mad
                                down hallways
blurring toward the vanishing point
I see the cloisters of my childhood
the anguish closing in
old anguish O my angel—
let us wrestle for control
                                down
the corridors of rigor am I
disciplined or cured?
a criminal or a patient
strapped and healing?
                                down
the balanced Roman arches drawn
in a whirl of vertigo I work
for equilibrium
                        I see
the architecture of sanity
the lines I draw so firmly
I may draw my spirit forth as
firm as live as Lazarus one morning

**The Wheat Field behind
St. Paul's Hospital
at the Fall of Day
with a Reaper**

Acres of rolling gold I now survey through bars,
the bumper crops of summer under sunset—
there in the midst a reaper battling all that bounty;
he is death, death as the great book of nature paints him
all but smiling . . . yes, I can almost feel him in me,
warm with the labor, laughing with the harvest—
gold for every stroke of his sickle, each crest he cuts.

The Cypress

black
I cannot
dead black
I cannot yet
get hold of
the dark the root
the tree of mourning
I cannot get to that
to the black that
is a color black
that grows to blue
I lack the skill
the sturdy growth
the layer on layer
brushing out and up
from the dead ends
the blue that grows
to green so tall
so somber climbing
columnar climbing
is what I need now
something beyond me
a lift   a dash
a ray on high
so far beyond me
and yet at times I
feel it within me
strange   deep
in the dark heart
of being   writhing
up like flame

I feel my ambition
cut to the cypress
the confirmation of
the tree of the dead
forever thrusting back
into life its dark
into points of fire
and rising yes I can
some days I think I can
unless the tree and I
black out together
the end may be
a star a sure
brilliance
glowing green
someday
we may
become
sheer
fire

The Starry Night

Long as I paint
I feel myself
less mad
the brush in my hand
a lightning rod to madness

But never ground that madness
execute it   ride the lightning up
from these benighted streets and steeple   up
with the cypress   look its black is burning green

I am that I am it cries
it lifts me up the nightfall   up
the cloudrack coiling like a dragon's flanks
a third of the stars of heaven wheeling in its wake
wheels in wheels around the moon that cradles round the sun

and if I can only trail these whirling eternal stars
with one sweep of the brush like Michael's sword if I can
cut the life out of the beast—safeguard the mother and the son
all heaven will hymn in conflagration blazing down
        the night the mountain ranges down
the claustrophobic valleys of the mad

                              Madness
    is what I have instead of heaven
    God deliver me—help me now deliver
    all this frenzy back into your hands
    our brushstrokes burning clearer into dawn

Self-Portrait   *i*

"I am the resurrection and the light"

My first day up, and the wraith of Vincent
looms before me . . .
he is a ghost that glows

Cheekbone, bone of the forehead
luminous
      flesh transparent
            green to ashen white
and the forelock like a halo waving gold

        A man who dreams great dreams, who sings
         as the nightingale sings, because it is his nature

His eyes edged in red
straining toward the horizon
           the far side of life
where the thunderheads of pain come clear with meaning

His sea-gown swarms around him
dragging him under—he is drowning
phosphorescent features struggling for air
for the blue the deepest darkest mineral cobalt
he can paint
        Infinity
           he can be
a blazing star in the depths of the azure heavens

    ii

Must be dreaming. "Better the sight of the eyes
than the wandering of desire."
Better to *look* at the morning star.
(Daubigny, Rousseau have depicted just that,
that majesty, so individual, heartbreaking—
you've no distaste for such feelings now.)

Star of the morning, first beheld through bars!
Pain, good for something.

                      Pain sharpens . . .
and they say (and they must be right)
it's hard to know yourself,
but it isn't easy, either, to paint yourself.
At work on two self-portraits at the moment.
That . . . you began the first day out of bed—
unreal, frenetic.

                This one will be simpler
if you can see it through, with their assistance.
We are one family here. Our golden rule:
"Bear with others that they may bear with you."

We understand each other very well,
the torpid, the raging, the old habitués
of the menagerie who separate the fighters.
Here in the room where we spend the interminable
rainy days, like a third-class waiting room
in some stagnant village, you can even find
respectable lunatics, always affecting a hat,
pince-nez, walkingstick, traveler's greatcoat.
A regular seaside resort. We are tourists
going nowhere, nodding . . .

                   the will goes numb—
at times you could take your life without remorse.
There comes a point, cowardly as you are,
when you have a right to protest—
suicide in self-defense . . .

                Soon perhaps, not yet.
"Better a living dog than a dead lion"—
and not here; there are so many here,
thank God, who also see strange sights,
who know the cries in the darkness.
Here, somehow, the horror of life recedes.
Understanding is half the battle.

                                        Apathy's the other.
Vegetating—terrifying. You must resist.
Healing comes, if one is desperate,
from cutting to the marrow. But the martyrs say,
"Resign yourself, surrender your own self-love."
Wisdom—the old anaesthetic, death to you.
You don't belong among the saints,
ready to live or die at the same moment.
You're anything but courageous in sorrow,
patient in pain. Save the patience for your work.
And pain?—must never collect in our hearts like water
in a swamp—
                Express it, let it out!
                                    It's cowardice,
yes, that makes you eat for two, work harder,
secrete yourself from the other patients,
fear relapse. You're trying to recover,
like a man who meant to drown himself
and finding the water too cold,
fights to regain the shore.
                            Palette
locked in your hand like a life preserver.
Master the stroke—what a wonderful thing *touch* is,
the stroke of the brush!   Work, work.

        iii

Lovely delirium of work . . .
and you always feel you are a traveler
going somewhere and to some destination and
if you tell yourself the destination does not exist,
that seems quite reasonable, highly likely in fact
and then you'll find the arts were simply dreams,
yourself, everything, nothing at all . . .
or with luck you may locate a native land
and see with the eyes of the child in the cradle,
not some world beyond, but the infinite in its eyes,

and you wish you could go home and see the family
gathered in one room like these . . . and at first
you felt repelled by them, harrowed to think
so many painters, Troyon, Marchal, Monticelli
and heaps more had ended up like this, and now
you are not afraid, and they might just as well
be touched by other illnesses, these artists,
you can see them assume their old serenity,
and is it a small thing to rediscover
the veterans of our profession? Not at all,
they even seem like kin, and you are grateful,
you begin to rediscover them all, the old masters,
Rembrandt and Hals, Daumier, Millet, Delacroix,
from the leanest black-and-white reproductions
of their work you begin to recreate them,
impersonate them, from your own early sketches
you begin to paint again, to gather a family, yes,
Père Tanguy, Roulin, my mother, the good earth . . .
I see them all return, all come drifting back,
a life's work gathered in one room, myself
in the midst but not my brother, strange,
I never painted you, Theo, never had to . . .
each self-portrait is of you, through you
I cultivate the best within myself
however guarded our tenderness may be . . .
remember, old man, the small emotions
are the great captains of our lives,
we obey them, without knowing it, in everything,
my painting, your fatherhood, our fatherland . . .
O Jerusalem, O Jerusalem—or rather, O Zundert, Zundert.
I wish I could go home now, Theo, must go north.

iv

The pulse picks up.   I come through older perhaps,
not sadder, though it often rushes back
at high tide of a painter's life—
the nostalgia, the ache for that real life,
impossible, out of reach.
                                        Worse, I often
lack the heart to throw myself into painting—
to get well for that. You're a cab horse, you know?
Hitched to the same creaking cab, hauling
coachfuls of people out to breathe the spring,
and you'd rather frisk in the meadows, drink the sun,
flanked by the other horses, mounting—free.
                                        Theo,
you're damn well right—"We'll have to battle
all our lives, starved for the oats of charity
doled out to the old horses in good stables."
Someone (I don't know who) called our condition
struck by death and immortality, both at once.
The load of iron you drag must be of use
to strangers, people you cannot know.
No matter. Believe in a new art,
that faith will never cheat us.
Good old Corot, remember? said the day he died,
"Last night I dreamed of landscapes, skies, all rose!"—
Well haven't they come, those skies of rose,
and yellow and green in the bargain?

We are aging, my brother, what of it?
Face it with a sort of northern phlegm.
That art to come is going to be so young—
give it our young blood (what's left of it)
and we may find some peace. More, that youth
crops up again in what we do, nothing lost,
the power to work is just another youth.

87

I begin again.   Return to myself.
Not the ghost of myself, not now.
What I see (mother will bear me out)
is more or less a peasant of Zundert,
Toon for instance, or Piet Prins,
though a peasant is more useful.
Still, keep plowing on your canvas.
Only the long slow labor ripens.
Simplicity, very difficult.
Must work, if you want to last,
with as few pretensions as a peasant.
Like a miner, bracing for the worst.
Ruin as many canvases as you keep.
Reason in cold blood—
try for the real, the possible—
back to the onslaught every morning,
things of this world.

                                    Dear brother,
I send you my own portrait today.
Look into it for a while, won't you?
Hold it beside the ones I did in Paris.
I look saner now.
I hope it will reassure you.
It is simple. It took some doing.
I have never felt more calm.

The wind whirls around me, look—
but through that storm I rise,
I plant my shoulders, head set
and the beard as red as earth,
the lips about to speak
filled with a silence leading on to action

and the lines of cheek and forehead firm
the eyes level, older but not sadder
open to anguish and exultation
simply alive
the eyes that see it all
and in the deluge may retain some peace

the eye that may be single, as I have prayed
that our whole body may also be full of light

the eye of the hurricane   steady clear and calm

I am such as I have seen myself to be

Olive Trees

I've worked in the olive grove this month.

Gauguin, Bernard, it's they who have maddened me
with their Christs in the Garden of Olives.
Flat allegories. Nothing really *observed*—
a dream, a nightmare, medieval tapestry.
Gives me the feeling of collapse, not progress.
Not to dream but to think, look closely;
that should be the assignment.
                                To shake them off
I knock about in the orchards, days and nights,
clear days and cool, crisp nights
at the end of summer, start of fall . . .
the wind in the olives rustles many secrets;
they are immensely old.

(These brief studies, I hope,
make up at least an attack on the problem.)

          Under the olive leaves the silver
                livid silver
          lifts in the wind and stirs to green,
          over the ochre soil I try to reach them—
                there are times they lead me on,
          I work myself into silver, straight into gold
          with the fresh shoots, ancient, ever-new
          these trees
                the revery and the restlessness
                    a hiss of misgiving in the wind
                            the roots of a lost affection
          the grip of old betrayals in the grain.

Am I mad or sane? A little of both, I hope.
I feel like a woodsman.
The long clean cuts of my lines
deliberate, stark as the old woodcuts,
distorted only to throw the olives in relief—

Up from the churning earth the bole and roots
heave upward, all is a struggling upward   always

Ramifying into the air the branches burl and writhe
so light aloft in the sky against the blue—
those mountains, weren't they blue?
Then make them blue, that's all

And heart-deep in the trees at end of summer
I can feel them sing, the cicadas singing
the shrill of the anguish rising
                                        a long dying fall
the cicadas shimmering through the ancient green

And I like a green olive tree in the house of God

The Road Menders

I must go north, go home,
reconstruct the way

heaps of sand
                    cut stone
                                and the huge trunks—
under the plane-trees I behold the town
torn up by excavation,
as if the Judgment Day had struck
and all come right at last. Women amble,
children play, and the men go at their labors,
dress the stones and set them . . . level-headed,
curbed,
the road paves north.

                        Break off—go *my* way,
train myself to the great trees of the south—
            molting out of their bark, lightning-white
                    limbs stabbing into the autumn skies afire
                        dying leaves erupting into fire!

Trees—Grand Armée on the march—
sweep me home with you.

Branch of an
Almond Tree in Blossom

Theo—a son!
I wish you'd called him Theo
after father—mother will be elated.
I launch right into a big birthday canvas,
big branches of almond blossoms against the sky
                        the lucid blue until it all
comes down on me once more
I gather the branches
blooming slowly
                        painstakingly
                firmer stroke by stroke
against the sky I plant them
branching finer
                                free
and the rind of the branches
                ringing silver
                                white blossoms
swaying against the manic azure
painting the almond boughs
before we fall again.
                        One day calm,
next day down like a brute.
So hard to fathom things like that,
but God, it is like that. The blooms
of early March are almost over.
I really have no luck.
                        But I have you
this spring, my nephew, here—
I hand these branches to you—
little Vincent, reach.

Reaper under a
Rising Sun

there is no god under heaven but the sun

the eye sees as the heart sees
and the hand must do the work

daybreak comes again
harrowing
cutting the furrows
                            violet scars
go Flanders yellow   helios yellow and
where they meet the lacerated earth goes green

my hand working the harvest
armies of winter wheat
                              spears glinting
fighting the rock wall that hugs the field
and over the olive groves and houses
over the blue shouldering hills
                                          the sun is rising
warm core of the morning   aurora gold and mounting
molten arms of the sun that burn the earth to life

searing white truth of the sun at high noon

sun at the temples pounding to explode

great sword of the sun

there is no god under heaven but the sun
cyclonic fire that burns me hurls me on

Portrait of Dr. Gachet

Country doctor, companion, last resort,
we work together daily, even now.

"Should the attacks become too much to bear,
I can relieve you, drug the intensity," he says,
"if only you can bear to be frank with me."

(Frank. Anything. Why not?
We've much in common. Flemings both,
socialists, mad for animals, free love,
though I wish he'd drop his pet scheme,
a Society for Mutual Autopsy.
                              We're very close,
our rooms like alchemists' garrets,
we turn anguish into art . . .
both addicted to painting,
Monticelli our hero,
old Pissarro introduced us.
                              Look at him,
pipe always lit, red hair, blue eyes—
strange resemblance between us . . .
his troubles great as mine, all right,
but a doctor's tools give him more defense,
or should—he's sicker about his patients
than I about my painting.
                              I'd trade him
job for job . . . *as* sick, that's certain.
Blind leading the blind to the same ditch!)

When I look at you, good doctor,
I see my double—
shade of the dead-born Vincent
growing old with me. Dear ghost,
can a touch of homeopathy help us both?
                                        Let me
paint you emerging from a deep blue valley
of depression
even your redingote is blue
    and the hand that props your head,
your face creased with the disenchantment of our time,
            but another hand is at the foxglove
(lavender digitalis, tonic for the heart)
your pale blue eyes, bright with anxiety
your hair more red than mine.

Let me catch your spirit—pressing fifty
you still project your latest study:
The Art of Living a Hundred Years.
Good luck!
Light apparition, so preserved,
neither you nor I will altogether die.

Pietà
(after Delacroix)

"Poor fighter, poor sufferer,"
my brother's words for me.
                              Self-pity—
I have to beat it down. But how, exactly?
Never know when the next attack will come.
How to suppress religion?
Down the cloisters of the sick it beckoned—
I abused my God . . . that lithograph of Delacroix's,
irredeemable sheets I flung in the paint and oil,
his *Pietà* in ruins.
                        Reconstruct it from memory.
Good technical exercise. Start with the hands,
there were four hands, four arms in the foreground—
mother and son, and the torsions of their bodies
almost impossible, draw them out—
painfully . . . no measurements—
into a great mutual gesture of despair.

Delacroix and I, we both discovered painting
when we no longer had breath or teeth.
Work into his work, strain for health,
the brain clearing, fingers firmer,
brush in the fingers going like a bow,
big bravura work—pure joy! I copy—
no, perform his masterwork of pain.

Genius of iridescent agony, Delacroix,
help me restore your lithograph with color.
I mortify before your model—
how to imitate my Christ? The bronze
of my forelock shadows his, the greatest artist:
stronger than all the others, spurning marble,
clay and paint, he worked in living flesh.

Living and yet immortal, Lord, revive me—
let me inhale the blue of Mary's cape
billowing hurricanes of hope, clothe me
in your cerements gold with morning—
mother and son, from all your sorrow
all renewal springs, the earth you touch
turns emerald as your hand that burgeons green

Crows over the
Wheat Field

I paint because I am
on the road the
interminable
mudchoked ruts
and each stroke
of the brush is one step
one furrow more I plow
through the eelgrass
struggle
           one more turn and
the road gives out
and the world is wheat and
rolling gold the rows come thick and fast
I cut my swath
              I am the reaper grim and gay
and the chaff is grating in my eyes
and if I can only reach the sky
I will be free at last
                 I will go out on the crest
I lunge and the world is open sweeping sky and
the great blue god oblivion lifts me up his thunderhead
he beats his azure wings and they are black I feel them closer
clashing tip to tip
                    to fling me down the wheatrows down the wheelruts
every blackbird's wing and pinion beating screaming blood against my skull
more black their strokes for all my brushstrokes slashing at their beaks

I Am Vincent
(*while painting the*
Church at Auvers)

i

A MIGHTY FORTRESS IS OUR GOD

night . . . thunderheads in the west and building

Our helper he amid the flood

the ramparts loom like a mineworks
Church—the masonry and the menace
threatening me from childhood

Still our ancient foe
Doth seek to work us woe

stand back, Vincent
put it into perspective . . .
first light on the rooflines
remember, it is a refuge—
try to make it so

The prince of darkness grim,
We tremble not for him

train the light on the transept
violet going orange
and the windows lucent   lifting

The Spirit and the gift are ours

to reinspire this aged hulk
fill it with breath the sky
the crashing blue

The body they may kill . . .
His kingdom is forever—

blue pure blue
and the ark of God amid the dwindling night
I steer like the old carpenter himself—
I shore our craft on this green bank of land
I am painting with the morning

breaking clear

I wish I could go home now.
Strange, painting this old church,
not home, not Holland . . .
and if I have my Luther on the brain
or exaggerate the apse a bit
it's only human—
                    (Like that Venus de Milo
years ago in Antwerp, and I told the professor,
"Damn it, a woman must have hips to hold a child!")
Big and broad, like the old church at Nuenen,
headstones nestled around it, tower rising;
I painted it many times, the more I did
the more ruinous it became,
the crown lopped, the graveyard gone to wrack.

I wanted to meet you in that graveyard, Theo,
settle our differences, many years ago.
Let's do it here before it is too late,
here where the paths diverge,
one to the graves, one with a woman strolling . . .
I'll try to make this churchyard more expressive,
less subdued.
                    It's absolutely mad, I know—
why I'd begun to resent you, Theo,
you and your support
(no good deed will ever go unpunished);
worse, the support drained, my work suffered . . .
now, thank God, I begin to paint again, my brother—
lecture you, but now in deadly earnest:
you are no simple dealer in Corots, Theo,
you are not among the dealers in men,
you choose your side—humanity.
                    Well and good,
but we've got to make our *pictures* speak,
tell and toll our feelings clear as bells.

I want this church to say You are my brother—
you and I, one flesh, one bone—we have shared
in the actual making of some canvases which,
come the deluge, just may stand their ground.
It is *our* work, you see, ours to pass along.
So if I risk my life for it, no matter;
if my reason goes because of it, Amen.

LET THE LITTLE CHILDREN COME TO ME
FOR OF SUCH IS THE KINGDOM OF GOD

Stone will crumble but the word remains,
weatherbeaten
                    family plot at Etten
the first Vincent's grave—
I think I'd like to die.
Suicide less repellent now.
"The act of a dishonest man," Millet?
I once refused to make murderers of the living,
now refuse to tax them any more,
you least of all, Theo.
                    Suicide . . .
the first flush of success is more unnerving—
like ramming the live end of your cigar
in your own mouth . . . self-consuming.
Must go out in my prime,
midsummer
                    midcareer
like Christ—
but not to that other kingdom;
must be active, always, like the reaper—
go where all those go who have the daring go.

Like the death's-head moth I did in hospital;
so rare, amazing colors, black shading off
into cloudy white, carmine, olive-green . . .
I killed the thing to paint it to the life—
I love the transformations of this world.

Life is probably round.

From grub to cockchafer,
caterpillar to chrysalis to butterfly
to one of the countless stars, after death,
but just as close as the black dots on the map
that go from Arles to Paris. This side of death
we see one hemisphere only, and beyond?
Life is round, not flat.
That other hemisphere, just another life.

And I used to think, I preached it years ago:

"Our journey extends from the loving breast
of our Mother on Earth to the arms
of our Father in Heaven."

I was wrong, mother,
forgive me. I come home to you forever.
Even here, behind this old village church,
here in a country grave where I set up my easel,
work with fury—a perfect avalanche of canvases,
70 paintings done in less than 70 days—
here I'd like to rest
for I can see the earth, mother,
the great plain of Auvers, darkening under storm,
green breast of land I see restored with every morning.

iii

I am Vincent of the scorched earth
                    by the fire from heaven raped
          and I will see the innocents screaming
tongues like knives to rend the breathless air
and the sultry bull of the earth enduring
                                             waiting

I am Vincent   I am vengeance
     peasant armies in phalanx moving out
carbines akimbo   massing like a breastwork

                                             I am war
     agony iridescent   lashing cross the eyes
soil in hemorrhage yes
   but the great poles molten laser blue
                    transfixing flood and thunder

I am Vincent of the victims
                         Miserere
whores   grotesques   old clowns old kings
     like characters out of Scripture yes
their flesh like opals
                    flesh cathedral windows

I am exultation yes I see this world reborn
through glass through sunburst
                              child-bird
     to mother-angel lifts her ram's-horn gold
exploding music yes chords crimson
                    as the bloodsack of creation
                                   I am Vincent

Library of Congress Cataloging in Publication Data

Fagles, Robert
  I, Vincent.

  (Princeton essays on the arts)
    1. Gogh, Vincent van, 1853-1890—Poetry.   I. Title.
PS3556.A33412   811'.5'4   77-85537
ISBN 0-691-06353-2
ISBN 0-691-01344-6 pbk.